# Leo Horoscope 2025

By
Thalia C. Astraea

# Table of Contents
# Leo (July 23 - August 22)

# Personality

**Leo** (July 23 – August 22), symbolized by the Lion, is a Fire sign ruled by the Sun, representing confidence, creativity, and warmth. Leos are known for their boldness, charisma, and natural leadership abilities. They shine brightest when they can express themselves authentically and inspire those around them. With a heart as big as their ambition, Leos are generous, loyal, and protective of their loved ones.

**Core Traits of Leo**

1. **Confident and Charismatic:** Leos naturally exude self-assurance and charm, making them magnetic in both social and professional settings.
2. **Creative and Expressive:** Their artistic flair and love for the spotlight inspire them to pursue endeavors in art, performance, or leadership.
3. **Generous and Warm-hearted:** Leos are known for their big hearts and willingness to support and uplift others.
4. **Loyal and Protective:** Once a Leo commits, their loyalty is unwavering. They are fiercely protective of their loved ones and will go to great lengths to ensure their happiness.
5. **Ambitious and Driven:** Leos thrive when they have clear goals and the opportunity to excel.

They are natural leaders who enjoy taking charge and inspiring others.

## Strengths of Leo

- **Leadership:** Leos have a commanding presence and the ability to motivate and guide others effectively.
- **Optimism:** Their sunny disposition and positive outlook make them resilient in the face of challenges.
- **Passion:** Leos pour their heart and soul into everything they do, from work to relationships.
- **Loyalty:** They are steadfast friends and partners who value trust and commitment.
- **Creativity:** Their imaginative minds and love for expression make them excellent innovators and performers.

## Weaknesses of Leo

- **Pride:** Their strong sense of self can sometimes come across as arrogance or stubbornness.
- **Attention-seeking:** Leos love to be in the spotlight, which may lead to conflict if they feel overlooked or unappreciated.
- **Impulsiveness:** Their fiery nature can lead to hasty decisions or overreactions.

- **Dominance:** Leo's natural leadership may come across as controlling if not balanced with empathy and collaboration.
- **Ego Sensitivity:** Criticism, even if constructive, can bruise their ego and lead to defensiveness.

## Leo in Relationships

*As Partners:*

Leos are passionate, romantic, and deeply committed in relationships. They thrive when they feel adored and appreciated, and in return, they shower their partners with affection and grand gestures.

- **Strengths in Love:** Loyal, passionate, and attentive to their partner's needs.
- **Challenges in Love:** Their need for attention and admiration may create tension if not balanced with mutual understanding.

*As Friends:*

Leos are lively and supportive friends who love to celebrate the successes of those they care about. Their enthusiasm and optimism make them the life of the party.

- **Strengths in Friendship:** Fun-loving, loyal, and always ready to help.

- **Challenges in Friendship:** They may dominate group dynamics or feel hurt if their efforts aren't reciprocated.

*As Family Members:*

Leos are protective and generous family members who take pride in nurturing and supporting their loved ones. They value family traditions and enjoy creating memorable experiences.

## Leo in Career and Professional Life

Leos excel in careers where they can express themselves, take charge, or make an impact. They are natural leaders who thrive in roles that allow them to showcase their talents and vision.

*Ideal Career Paths:*

- **Leadership and Management:** Their charisma and decisiveness make them excellent managers, CEOs, or team leaders.
- **Creative Arts:** Acting, design, music, or writing aligns with their love for self-expression.
- **Public Relations and Marketing:** Their natural charm and ability to inspire make them effective communicators.

- **Entrepreneurship:** Leos' ambition and creativity help them turn their visions into successful ventures.
- **Teaching or Mentoring:** Their enthusiasm and leadership qualities make them inspiring educators or mentors.

*Workplace Traits:*

- **Strengths:** Enthusiastic, inspiring, and goal-oriented. Leos bring energy and innovation to their teams.
- **Challenges:** They may struggle with accepting feedback or sharing the spotlight.

## Leo and Personal Growth

To reach their full potential, Leos can benefit from balancing their confidence with humility and focusing on collaboration.

*Tips for Personal Growth:*

1. **Embrace Feedback:** Learn to accept constructive criticism and use it to grow.
2. **Balance Confidence with Empathy:** Focus on listening and valuing others' contributions.
3. **Manage Impulsivity:** Practice patience and think through decisions before acting.

4. **Cultivate Humility:** Acknowledge the efforts of others and share credit for success.
5. **Nurture Inner Peace:** Engage in mindfulness practices to stay grounded and centered.

## Leo Compatibility

- **Best Matches:** Aries, Sagittarius, Libra, and Gemini—these signs appreciate Leo's energy, passion, and charisma.
- **Challenging Matches:** Taurus and Scorpio, as their fixed nature, may clash with Leo's need for flexibility and attention.

## Conclusion

Leos are vibrant, passionate, and charismatic individuals who light up every room they enter. While their bold nature and love for the spotlight can sometimes be overwhelming, their warmth, loyalty, and creativity make them beloved friends, partners, and leaders. By balancing their strengths with self-awareness and collaboration, Leos can achieve remarkable success and fulfillment in every aspect of life.

# Introduce

For Leo (July 23 – August 22), 2025 is a year of transformation, personal achievement, and creative exploration. Ruled by the Sun, Leos naturally exudes charisma and confidence, and this year will amplify those traits while also encouraging self-reflection and balance. The celestial alignments in 2025 will present opportunities for Leos to expand their horizons, strengthen relationships, and pursue bold goals.

Whether in love, career, or personal development, this year is about harnessing your natural talents while remaining open to new possibilities. Let's take an in-depth look at what 2025 holds for Leos.

## Overall Energy for Leo in 2025

The year begins with Jupiter in Taurus, emphasizing career growth and financial stability. This energy supports steady progress, helping you lay the groundwork for lasting success. By mid-year, as Jupiter transitions into Gemini, you'll feel inspired to expand your social circle, explore creative ventures, and embrace new learning opportunities.

Meanwhile, Saturn in Pisces will push you to focus on emotional depth and personal transformation. This influence encourages you to work through unresolved issues and strengthen your emotional resilience. Uranus in Taurus continues to bring surprises in your professional life, challenging you to adapt and innovate.

Leos are naturally bold and dynamic, and 2025 encourages you to take the lead while maintaining balance and humility.

## Career and Ambition

2025 offers tremendous potential for Leos to shine in their professional life. Jupiter's influence in Taurus during the first half of the year brings stability and rewards for your hard work, while Uranus ensures that innovation and adaptability remain key themes.

- **Key Opportunities:** The first half of the year is ideal for pursuing promotions, launching new projects, or establishing long-term professional goals. Networking and collaboration will also play a significant role in your success.
- **Challenges:** Unexpected changes in the workplace or industry may require quick thinking and flexibility. While Leos excels under pressure, staying grounded and organized will be essential.

**Tips for Career Success in 2025:**

1. Use the steady energy of early 2025 to build a strong professional foundation.
2. Leverage your creativity and leadership skills to stand out in team projects.
3. Stay open to feedback and be prepared to adapt to changing circumstances.

## Wealth and Finances

Financial growth and stability are central themes for Leo in 2025. Jupiter in Taurus supports disciplined financial planning, making this a great time to focus on investments, savings, and long-term security.

- **Key Opportunities:** The first half of the year may bring financial rewards through promotions, new ventures, or successful investments. Creative projects could also yield additional income.
- **Challenges:** Impulsive spending or overconfidence in financial decisions could disrupt your stability.

**Tips for Financial Success in 2025:**

1. Create a detailed budget and stick to it, even when tempted by luxury purchases.
2. Reassess your investment strategies and seek professional advice if needed.

3. Focus on saving for future goals rather than short-term indulgences.

## Love and Relationships

In 2025, Leo's love life will thrive with warmth, passion, and deep connections. Venus will bring harmony to your relationships, while the influence of Saturn encourages emotional growth and maturity.

- **For Singles:** This year is ideal for meeting someone special, especially during social gatherings or creative events. You'll attract partners who appreciate your confidence and zest for life, but meaningful connections will come from authenticity and emotional depth.
- **For Those in Relationships:** Focus on strengthening trust and communication with your partner. Plan shared experiences to rekindle romance and deepen your bond. Challenges may arise during Venus retrograde periods, but these moments will offer opportunities for growth and understanding.

## Challenges in Love:

- Your natural need for attention may create tension if not balanced with mutual appreciation.

- Saturn's influence may bring unresolved emotional issues to the surface, requiring patience and empathy.

**Tips for Love and Relationships in 2025:**

1. Practice active listening and be open to compromise in your relationships.
2. Use challenging moments as opportunities to grow closer to your partner.
3. Balance passion with emotional intimacy to create a fulfilling love life.

**Health and Wellness**

Health is a key focus for Leo in 2025, particularly during Saturn's transit through Pisces, which encourages emotional and physical self-care.

- **Physical Health:** The disciplined energy of Saturn will inspire you to adopt healthier habits, such as regular exercise, balanced nutrition, and better sleep routines.
- **Mental and Emotional Health:** Reflective practices like journaling, meditation, or therapy will help you process emotions and maintain balance amidst life's demands.

## Challenges in Health:

Stress from balancing work, relationships, and personal goals may lead to fatigue if not managed effectively.

## Tips for Health and Wellness in 2025:

1. Prioritize self-care and avoid overcommitting to obligations.
2. Incorporate mindfulness practices into your daily routine to stay centered.
3. Make time for hobbies and activities that bring you joy and relaxation.

## Personal Growth and Spirituality

2025 is a year of personal transformation for Leo. Saturn in Pisces encourages introspection and emotional resilience, helping you align with your higher purpose. This is a time to let go of past fears or limitations and embrace a more authentic version of yourself.

- **Key Themes:** Self-discovery, emotional healing, and cultivating inner peace will be central to your growth.

- **Opportunities for Growth:** Spiritual practices, creative hobbies, or travel experiences will expand your horizons and provide new perspectives.

## Tips for Personal Growth in 2025:

1. Use journaling or meditation to explore your emotions and clarify your goals.
2. Stay open to feedback and view challenges as opportunities for growth.
3. Focus on building resilience by embracing change and stepping out of your comfort zone.

## Key Dates for Leo in 2025

- **February 14:** A Full Moon in Leo highlights your strengths and brings clarity to your goals.
- **July 23 – August 22:** The Sun in Leo energizes you, making this your time to shine in all areas of life.
- **November 13:** A New Moon in Scorpio inspires introspection and emotional growth.

## Challenges for Leo in 2025

- Balancing your natural desire for attention with the needs of others in your personal and professional life.

- Managing stress and avoiding burnout by pacing yourself and maintaining a healthy work-life balance.
- Letting go of old habits or beliefs that no longer serve your growth.

**Conclusion**

2025 is a dynamic and empowering year for Leo. By embracing your natural charisma and creativity while staying open to personal growth, you'll achieve remarkable success and build meaningful connections. Focus on maintaining balance, nurturing relationships, and aligning with your authentic self to make this year truly unforgettable.

Leo, the world is your stage in 2025—step into the spotlight with confidence and let your brilliance shine!

# January

January 2025 is a month of focus, determination, and careful planning for Leo. The new year begins with the Sun in Capricorn, emphasizing discipline, organization, and long-term goals. This is a time to lay the groundwork for success in your personal and professional life. With Mercury retrograde during the early part of the month, it's a good idea to double-check details and avoid rushing into decisions.

## *Work*

January is a productive month for Leo, with opportunities to establish a solid foundation for the year ahead.

- **Opportunities:** Capricorn Energy encourages strategic planning and steady progress in your career. Collaborative efforts and networking will enhance your professional growth.
- **Challenges:** Mercury retrograde in the early weeks may cause delays or miscommunications in the workplace.

**Advice:** Use the first half of the month to reassess your goals and focus on organization. By mid-January, take action on well-thought-out plans.

<u>*Finance*</u>

Your financial outlook in January requires mindful planning and cautious decision-making.

- **Opportunities:** Reassessing your budget and creating a savings plan will help you build long-term financial stability. Small financial gains may come from past efforts.
- **Challenges:** Avoid impulsive spending or making significant financial commitments during Mercury retrograde.

**Advice:** Focus on saving and stick to your budget. Delaying major purchases until after mid-month will ensure better outcomes.

<u>*Love*</u>

January brings a grounded and reflective tone to your love life. Open communication and thoughtful gestures will strengthen your connections.

- **For Singles:** Use this time to reflect on what you want in a partner. Later in the month, you may meet someone through work or social events.
- **For Those in Relationships:** Focus on building trust and addressing any unresolved issues with compassion and understanding.

**Advice:** Be patient in your interactions and focus on quality time. Use this month to nurture emotional intimacy and create a strong foundation in your relationships.

## *Health*

Health-wise, January encourages Leo to prioritize balance and stress management.

- **Strengths:** You'll feel motivated to establish healthier routines, such as regular exercise and improved eating habits.
- **Challenges:** Stress or fatigue from professional and personal responsibilities may impact your energy levels if not managed properly.

**Advice:** Incorporate relaxation techniques like yoga, meditation, or deep breathing into your routine. Focus on hydration and ensure you're getting enough rest.

## *Be Careful*

- **Overcommitment:** Avoid taking on too many responsibilities at once, as this could lead to unnecessary stress.
- **Miscommunication:** Mercury retrograde may cause misunderstandings; double-check details in work and personal matters.

- **Impulsive Decisions:** Delay major commitments or purchases until the retrograde ends mid-month.

## *Advice*

1. **Plan Strategically:** Use the Capricorn energy to set clear, realistic goals and create a roadmap for the year ahead.
2. **Strengthen Relationships:** Focus on meaningful connections and build trust through open communication.
3. **Prioritize Self-Care:** Balance productivity with downtime to maintain your energy and well-being.

## *Additional Tips*

- **Lucky Days:** January 10, 18, and 26 – Perfect for thoughtful decision-making, networking, or creative projects.
- **Lucky Color:** Gold – This color symbolizes success, confidence, and positivity.
- **Affirmation for January:** *"I align my actions with my goals, creating a strong foundation for growth and success."*

January 2025 sets the stage for a productive and fulfilling year for Leo. By staying focused, organized, and mindful, you'll navigate this period with confidence and clarity.

# February

February 2025 is a month of connection, creativity, and progress for Leo. With the Sun in Aquarius during the first half of the month, your focus will be on relationships, collaboration, and innovative thinking. As the Sun transitions into Pisces later in February, the energy becomes more introspective and emotionally enriching. This balance between external action and inner reflection makes February a time of growth and connection.

## *Work*

February offers opportunities for Leo to collaborate and shine in their professional life.

- **Opportunities:** Networking and teamwork will play a significant role in your success. Mid-month may bring opportunities to pitch ideas, take on leadership roles, or explore creative projects.
- **Challenges:** You may encounter differing opinions or resistance to change in group settings. Stay diplomatic and patient.

**Advice:** Focus on fostering strong professional relationships and communicating your ideas. Use the introspective energy of late February to refine your long-term goals.

*__Finance__*

Your financial outlook in February encourages disciplined spending and thoughtful planning.

- **Opportunities:** Creative ventures or side projects may bring additional income. This is also a good time to revisit your budget and ensure it aligns with your priorities.
- **Challenges:** Avoid overspending on social events or luxury items, especially during moments of celebration or stress.

**Advice:** Stick to a budget and focus on saving for future goals. Delay major financial decisions until you've had time to consider all options.

*__Love__*

February is a warm and romantic month for Leo, with Venus fostering connection and harmony in your relationships.

- **For Singles:** You may meet someone intriguing through social gatherings, work events, or mutual friends. Your natural charm will attract admirers, but focus on building genuine connections.
- **For Those in Relationships:** This is a great time to nurture emotional intimacy and plan special

moments with your partner. Open communication and shared activities will strengthen your bond.

**Advice:** Be authentic and open about your feelings. Use the Pisces energy later in the month to deepen emotional connections and build trust.

## *Health*

Health-wise, February encourages Leo to focus on balance and self-care amidst a busy social and professional schedule.

- **Strengths:** You'll feel motivated to stay active and maintain healthy habits. Creative hobbies or physical activities like dancing or yoga will help keep you energized.
- **Challenges:** Social commitments or work-related stress may impact your energy levels if not managed effectively.

**Advice:** Incorporate relaxation techniques into your routine to stay grounded. Focus on hydration, nutrition, and getting adequate rest to maintain overall well-being.

### _Be Careful_

- **Overcommitting:** Avoid taking on too many responsibilities or social obligations, as this could lead to stress or burnout.
- **Impulsiveness:** Think carefully before making significant financial or personal decisions.
- **Neglecting Rest:** Balance your active schedule with downtime to recharge and avoid fatigue.

### _Advice_

1. **Collaborate and Connect:** Use the dynamic Aquarius energy to build relationships and work effectively in team settings.
2. **Reflect and Refine:** Embrace the introspective Pisces energy to align with your long-term goals and emotional needs.
3. **Prioritize Balance:** Maintain a healthy balance between socializing, productivity, and self-care to stay energized and focused.

### _Additional Tips_

- **Lucky Days:** February 9, 16, and 28 – Ideal for networking, creative projects, or deepening relationships.
- **Lucky Color:** Royal Blue – This color enhances clarity, confidence, and communication.

- **Affirmation for February:** *"I balance connection and reflection, creating harmony and success in all areas of my life."*

February 2025 is a month of growth and connection for Leo. By focusing on meaningful relationships, thoughtful planning, and self-care, you'll navigate this dynamic period with confidence and grace.

# March

March 2025 is a month of transformation, self-discovery, and emotional depth for Leo. With the Sun in Pisces for most of the month, the focus shifts to introspection, creativity, and strengthening emotional connections. As the Sun transitions into Aries later in March, the energy becomes bold, dynamic, and action-oriented, encouraging you to take the lead and pursue your goals with confidence.

## *Work*

March presents Leo with opportunities to balance creativity and ambition in their professional life.

- **Opportunities:** The Pisces energy in the first half of the month supports brainstorming, creative problem-solving, and refining your long-term vision. Later in March, Aries' influence brings courage and motivation, making it the perfect time to launch new projects or take on leadership roles.
- **Challenges:** Emotional distractions or self-doubt early in the month may slow your progress. Focus on clarity and avoid overthinking decisions.

**Advice:** Use the reflective energy of early March to strategize and the dynamic energy of late March to act decisively. Stay open to feedback from colleagues or mentors.

## *Finance*

Your financial outlook in March highlights careful planning and the potential for moderate growth.

- **Opportunities:** Creative ventures or collaborations may bring additional income. This is also a good time to reassess your investments and savings strategies.
- **Challenges:** Avoid impulsive spending, especially on items or experiences that don't align with your long-term financial goals.

**Advice:** Focus on building financial stability. Use the bold Aries energy later in the month to make thoughtful decisions about income-generating opportunities.

## *Love*

March brings emotional depth and warmth to your love life, with Venus encouraging connection and intimacy.

- **For Singles:** This is a great month to meet someone special, particularly through creative or spiritual pursuits. Emotional and intellectual connections will feel especially significant.

- **For Those in Relationships:** Focus on nurturing emotional intimacy and resolving past misunderstandings. Planning special moments or trips together will help deepen your bond.

**Advice:** Be vulnerable and authentic in your interactions. Use the bold energy of late March to express your feelings and strengthen your relationships.

## *Health*

Health-wise, March encourages Leo to focus on emotional and physical well-being through mindfulness and balance.

- **Strengths:** Your motivation to maintain healthy routines, such as regular exercise and balanced nutrition, will be strong. Activities like yoga, swimming, or creative hobbies will help you stay centered.
- **Challenges:** Emotional stress from work or personal matters may impact your energy levels if not addressed.

**Advice:** Practice mindfulness techniques, prioritize sleep, and avoid overexertion. Take breaks to recharge and maintain a healthy work-life balance.

## _Be Careful_

- **Overthinking:** Avoid getting stuck in emotional analysis during the reflective Pisces energy of early March. Stay grounded in the present.
- **Impulsive Actions:** Don't rush into decisions, especially financial or professional ones, during the Aries energy of late March.
- **Neglecting Self-Care:** Balance your ambitious goals with downtime to avoid burnout.

## _Advice_

1. **Reflect and Plan:** Use early March to refine your goals and align with your emotional and professional priorities.
2. **Act with Confidence:** Embrace the bold Aries energy of late March to take decisive steps toward your aspirations.
3. **Nurture Relationships:** Invest time in deepening connections with loved ones and addressing unresolved issues.

## _Additional Tips_

- **Lucky Days:** March 10, 18, and 28 — Ideal for decision-making, creative pursuits, or strengthening relationships.

- **Lucky Color:** Fiery Orange – This color enhances creativity, courage, and positivity.
- **Affirmation for March:** *"I embrace transformation and bold action, creating harmony and progress in my life."*

March 2025 is a month of growth and empowerment for Leo. By balancing introspection with action and prioritizing meaningful connections, you'll set the stage for a dynamic and fulfilling year ahead.

# April

April 2025 is a month of ambition, adventure, and forward momentum for Leo. With the Sun in Aries during the first part of the month, the energy is dynamic and bold, inspiring you to pursue your goals with confidence and enthusiasm. As the Sun transitions into Taurus later in April, the focus shifts to grounding, stability, and building lasting foundations for the future. This month offers opportunities to balance your fiery ambition with practical planning and thoughtful reflection.

## *Work*

April presents Leo with opportunities to lead and innovate in their professional life.

- **Opportunities:** The bold Aries energy inspires you to take charge of projects, present ideas, and pursue leadership roles. Mid-month is ideal for launching new ventures or seeking mentorship.
- **Challenges:** Balancing your enthusiasm with practicality may be challenging early in the month. Avoid rushing decisions or taking on more than you can handle.

**Advice:** Use the steady Taurus energy later in the month to ground your ambitions and refine your strategies.

Stay focused on long-term goals while maintaining a collaborative attitude.

## _Finance_

Your financial outlook in April emphasizes disciplined spending and opportunities for gradual growth.

- **Opportunities:** Creative projects or investments may show promising returns. This is also a good time to review your financial goals and adjust your budget as needed.
- **Challenges:** Impulsive purchases or spending on luxury items could strain your finances if not managed carefully.

**Advice:** Focus on financial stability by prioritizing savings and avoiding unnecessary expenses. Consider consulting a financial advisor for long-term planning.

## _Love_

April brings warmth and excitement to your love life, with Venus highlighting connection and harmony.

- **For Singles:** This is a great time to meet someone who shares your passions and values. Social gatherings or adventurous activities may lead to meaningful connections.

- **For Those in Relationships:** Focus on deepening emotional intimacy and planning special moments with your partner. The Taurus energy later in the month encourages nurturing and stability in your relationship.

**Advice:** Be authentic and open about your feelings. Use the adventurous Aries energy to explore new experiences together and the grounding Taurus energy to strengthen your bond.

## *Health*

Health-wise, April encourages Leo to maintain balance and stay active while managing stress.

- **Strengths:** Your energy levels will be high, especially during the Aries influence. Outdoor activities, fitness routines, or creative hobbies will help you stay energized.
- **Challenges:** Overexertion or neglecting rest may lead to fatigue if not managed effectively.

**Advice:** Incorporate relaxation techniques like yoga, meditation, or deep breathing into your routine. Ensure you're maintaining a balanced diet, staying hydrated, and getting adequate sleep.

## *Be Careful*

- **Impulsiveness:** Avoid making hasty decisions in your work or finances, especially during the high-energy Aries season.
- **Overcommitment:** Don't overextend yourself by taking on too many responsibilities or social obligations.
- **Neglecting Self-Care:** Balance your ambitious goals with downtime to recharge and maintain well-being.

## *Advice*

1. **Take Bold Steps:** Use the Aries energy to pursue your ambitions with courage and enthusiasm.
2. **Focus on Stability:** Embrace the Taurus energy later in the month to ground your plans and ensure long-term success.
3. **Nurture Relationships:** Strengthen personal and professional connections through open communication and mutual support.

## *Additional Tips*

- **Lucky Days:** April 12, 20, and 30 – Ideal for making decisions, starting projects, or nurturing relationships.

- **Lucky Color:** Golden Yellow – This color symbolizes optimism, success, and vitality.
- **Affirmation for April:** *"I balance bold action with thoughtful planning, creating harmony and success in all areas of my life."*

April 2025 is a month of dynamic progress and stability for Leo. By balancing your ambition with practicality and focusing on meaningful connections, you'll set the stage for lasting growth and fulfillment.

# May

May 2025 is a month of grounding, reflection, and steady progress for Leo. With the Sun in Taurus during the first part of the month, the focus is on building stability, nurturing relationships, and consolidating your achievements. As the Sun transitions into Gemini later in May, the energy shifts to curiosity, communication, and expanding your social circle. This blend of energies encourages the balance between thoughtful planning and dynamic exploration.

## *Work*

May is a productive and stabilizing month for Leo's professional life.

- **Opportunities:** Taurus Energy supports long-term planning, organization, and refining ongoing projects. Mid-month is ideal for networking or presenting your ideas to influential people.
- **Challenges:** You may feel tempted to rush decisions or multitask excessively as the Gemini energy picks up. Avoid spreading yourself too thin.

**Advice:** Use the grounded energy of early May to focus on important details and the dynamic energy of late May to explore new opportunities and collaborations.

<u>*Finance*</u>

Your financial outlook in May emphasizes stability and thoughtful planning.

- **Opportunities:** You may see steady progress in financial ventures that started earlier this year. Creative or collaborative efforts could bring in additional income.
- **Challenges:** Avoid impulsive spending on luxury items or entertainment, particularly as social opportunities increase later in the month.

**Advice:** Stick to your budget and focus on saving for long-term goals. Reassess your financial strategies to ensure they align with your priorities.

<u>*Love*</u>

May is a warm and harmonious month for Leo's love life, with Venus fostering connection and emotional depth.

- **For Singles:** This is a great time to meet someone special through mutual friends, professional settings, or social events. Conversations will flow easily, making it an excellent time for building connections.

- **For Those in Relationships:** Focus on nurturing emotional intimacy and planning quality time with your partner. Late May is ideal for introducing more lighthearted fun into your relationship.

**Advice:** Use Taurus energy to deepen your emotional bond and Gemini energy to explore new ways to keep your relationship exciting and fresh.

## *Health*

Health-wise, May encourages Leo to maintain balance and stay consistent with wellness routines.

- **Strengths:** The steady Taurus energy will inspire you to focus on physical fitness, mindful eating, and relaxation techniques.
- **Challenges:** Increased social activity later in the month may disrupt your routines or lead to overindulgence.

**Advice:** Prioritize self-care by scheduling regular downtime. Stay hydrated, maintain a balanced diet, and incorporate relaxation techniques like meditation or yoga.

## *Be Careful*

- **Overindulgence:** Avoid overcommitting to social events or indulging in unhealthy habits during celebrations.
- **Neglecting Details:** Don't overlook important details in your work or financial planning.
- **Impulsiveness:** Resist the urge to act on impulse, particularly in financial or personal decisions.

## *Advice*

1. **Focus on Stability:** Use the Taurus energy of early May to solidify your foundations and build toward your long-term goals.
2. **Embrace Social Energy:** As Gemini season begins, explore new opportunities to expand your network and engage with others.
3. **Balance Work and Play:** Stay grounded while enjoying the lighter, more adventurous energy later in the month.

## *Additional Tips*

- **Lucky Days:** May 8, 17, and 27 – Ideal for making thoughtful decisions, pursuing creative projects, or strengthening relationships.
- **Lucky Color:** Emerald Green – This color symbolizes growth, balance, and abundance.

- **Affirmation for May:** *"I create stability and connection, aligning my actions with my dreams and values."*

May 2025 is a month of progress and connection for Leo. By focusing on thoughtful planning, meaningful relationships, and personal growth, you'll set the stage for success and fulfillment in the months ahead.

# June

June 2025 is a month of self-expression, social engagement, and preparation for the dynamic period ahead. With the Sun in Gemini for most of the month, your energy will focus on communication, curiosity, and expanding your horizons. As the Sun transitions into Cancer later in June, you'll feel a shift toward introspection and emotional connection. This is a time to balance external activities with internal reflection, ensuring you're ready for the opportunities that come with your birthday season in July.

## *Work*

June offers opportunities for Leo to expand their influence and refine their professional goals.

- **Opportunities:** Networking, public speaking, and collaborative projects will bring recognition and open doors to new opportunities. Mid-month is especially favorable for sharing ideas or attending events that connect you with influential individuals.
- **Challenges:** Balancing your eagerness to try new things with the need to follow through on current responsibilities may feel challenging.

**Advice:** Stay organized and focused. Use the Gemini energy to explore new ideas and the Cancer energy later in the month to ground your plans in practicality.

## *Finance*

Your financial outlook in June emphasizes cautious spending and seizing new opportunities for income growth.

- **Opportunities:** Creative ventures or side projects may offer financial rewards. This is also a good time to research investment opportunities or revisit your budget.
- **Challenges:** Impulse purchases or overspending on social events may strain your budget if not managed carefully.

**Advice:** Focus on long-term financial security. Avoid unnecessary expenses and think carefully before committing to major purchases.

## *Love*

June is a warm and sociable month for Leo's love life, with Venus enhancing connection and harmony.

- **For Singles:** You'll attract attention with your charisma and wit, making it an excellent time to meet new people. Social events and group activities may lead to romantic opportunities.

- **For Those in Relationships:** Focus on open communication and shared experiences with your partner. Plan activities that allow you to connect emotionally and create memorable moments together.

**Advice:** Balance lighthearted fun with deeper emotional connections. Use the introspective Cancer energy later in the month to strengthen your bond.

## *Health*

Health-wise, June encourages Leo to focus on both physical activity and mental well-being.

- **Strengths:** Your energy levels will be high, especially during the Gemini season. Outdoor activities, fitness routines, or creative hobbies will keep you motivated and energized.
- **Challenges:** Overexertion or neglecting rest may lead to fatigue if you don't maintain a balanced schedule.

**Advice:** Incorporate relaxation techniques into your routine, such as meditation, journaling, or light exercise. Ensure you're getting adequate sleep and staying hydrated to maintain your overall well-being.

- **Overcommitting:** Avoid taking on too many responsibilities or social engagements, as this could lead to stress or burnout.
- **Emotional Overload:** Don't ignore your need for downtime, especially as Cancer season encourages introspection.
- **Impulsive Spending:** Keep an eye on your budget to ensure you're staying on track with your financial goals.

## _Advice_

1. **Expand Your Network:** Use the social energy of Gemini season to connect with others and explore new opportunities.
2. **Reflect and Recharge:** Embrace the introspective Cancer energy to realign your goals and nurture emotional connections.
3. **Maintain Balance:** Stay grounded by balancing external activities with self-care and reflection.

## _Additional Tips_

- **Lucky Days:** June 7, 16, and 25 — Perfect for networking, pursuing creative projects, or deepening relationships.

- **Lucky Color:** Royal Blue – This color symbolizes confidence, clarity, and communication.
- **Affirmation for June:** *"I embrace connection and reflection, creating harmony and growth in my life."*

June 2025 is a month of exploration and balance for Leo. By focusing on your social connections, creative pursuits, and emotional well-being, you'll navigate this dynamic period with confidence and set the stage for an exciting summer.

# July

July 2025 is your month to shine, Leo! With the Sun entering your sign mid-month, you'll feel a surge of energy, confidence, and inspiration. This is your time to embrace the spotlight, focus on your goals, and nurture your relationships. The early part of the month, under the influence of Cancer, encourages reflection and emotional growth, while the Leo season brings boldness and dynamic opportunities.

## *Work*

July offers a blend of introspection and action, helping Leos achieve professional success.

- **Opportunities:** The first half of the month is ideal for reflecting on your career goals and planning your next moves. As the Sun moves into Leo, your natural charisma will attract attention and open doors for leadership roles or creative projects.
- **Challenges:** Balancing the need for reflection with your desire to act immediately may feel challenging. Avoid rushing into decisions without thorough planning.

**Advice:** Use the Cancer energy early in the month to refine your strategies, then step into the spotlight during Leo season to showcase your skills and take decisive action.

## *Finance*

Your financial situation in July emphasizes growth and thoughtful decision-making.

- **Opportunities:** Mid-month brings potential financial gains from past efforts, side projects, or creative endeavors. Use this time to reassess your budget and plan for long-term goals.
- **Challenges:** Avoid overspending on luxury items or celebratory activities during Leo season.

**Advice:** Maintain a balance between enjoying your success and securing your financial future. Delay major purchases until you've thoroughly considered their impact.

## *Love*

July is a passionate and exciting month for Leo's love life, with Venus enhancing romance and connection.

- **For Singles:** Your natural charm and confidence will attract admirers, making it a great time to meet new people. Social events, creative activities, or travel may lead to promising connections.

- **For Those in Relationships:** Focus on rekindling the spark in your relationship with thoughtful gestures and shared adventures. The energy of Leo season inspires passion and romance.

**Advice:** Be authentic and open about your feelings. Celebrate your relationships while ensuring you're also attentive to your partner's needs.

### *Health*

Health-wise, July encourages Leo to stay active and prioritize self-care.

- **Strengths:** Your energy levels will peak mid-month, making it an excellent time for fitness activities, outdoor adventures, or trying new wellness routines.
- **Challenges:** Overexertion or neglecting rest during the excitement of Leo season may lead to fatigue.

**Advice:** Balance your high-energy pursuits with adequate downtime. Incorporate mindfulness practices like yoga or meditation to maintain emotional and physical well-being.

## _Be Careful_

- **Overconfidence:** Avoid letting your natural confidence turn into arrogance, especially in professional or personal interactions.
- **Impulsiveness:** Think carefully before making major decisions, particularly in financial or career matters.
- **Neglecting Balance:** Don't let the excitement of Leo season overshadow the importance of reflection and self-care.

## _Advice_

1. **Embrace the Spotlight:** Use the bold energy of Leo season to pursue your ambitions and take charge in personal and professional matters.
2. **Balance Action with Reflection:** Incorporate the introspective Cancer energy to ensure your actions align with your long-term goals.
3. **Celebrate Your Relationships:** Invest time in nurturing connections with loved ones and expressing gratitude for their support.

## _Additional Tips_

- **Lucky Days:** July 10, 19, and 29 – Perfect for making decisions, pursuing creative projects, or celebrating special moments.

- **Lucky Color:** Gold – This color enhances confidence, success, and positivity.
- **Affirmation for July:** *"I shine with confidence and purpose, creating joy and success in every area of my life."*

July 2025 is a month of empowerment and celebration for Leo. By focusing on your goals, nurturing your relationships, and prioritizing self-care, you'll navigate this vibrant period with grace and excitement.

# August

August 2025 is a dynamic and empowering month for Leo, with the Sun shining brightly in your sign for the first few weeks. This is a time to celebrate your achievements, showcase your talents, and embrace the spotlight. As the Sun transitions into Virgo later in the month, the focus shifts toward grounding, planning, and refining your goals. Balance celebration with thoughtful action to make the most of this vibrant period.

## *Work*

August offers opportunities for Leo to lead, innovate, and build on recent successes.

- **Opportunities:** The high-energy Leo season encourages bold moves, creative initiatives, and pursuing leadership roles. The Virgo energy later in the month supports detailed planning and long-term strategies.
- **Challenges:** Overconfidence or a lack of attention to detail early in the month may lead to minor setbacks.

**Advice:** Use the bold energy of Leo season to take risks and the grounded Virgo influence to solidify your progress. Stay humble and focus on collaboration.

<u>*Finance*</u>

Your financial outlook in August is stable, with potential for growth if you manage resources wisely.

- **Opportunities:** Financial gains may come from past efforts, creative projects, or unexpected opportunities. Use this time to reassess your savings and investment strategies.
- **Challenges:** Avoid overspending on luxury items, entertainment, or celebrations during the first half of the month.

**Advice:** Maintain a balanced approach to spending. Focus on saving and think long-term, especially as Virgo season begins.

<u>*Love*</u>

August is a passionate and romantic month for Leo, with Venus enhancing emotional connection and intimacy.

- **For Singles:** You'll exude confidence and charm, making it an excellent time to meet new people. Social events or creative activities may lead to meaningful encounters.
- **For Those in Relationships:** Focus on reigniting passion and creating memorable moments with

your partner. Shared activities and thoughtful gestures will strengthen your bond.

**Advice:** Celebrate your relationships while also ensuring mutual understanding and support. Use the Virgo energy later in the month to address any lingering issues with patience and care.

## *Health*

Health-wise, August encourages Leo to balance activity and rest to maintain overall well-being.

- **Strengths:** Your energy levels will be high, making it a great time to pursue fitness goals, and outdoor activities, or try new wellness routines.
- **Challenges:** Overexertion during the excitement of Leo season may lead to fatigue or minor health concerns.

**Advice:** Prioritize self-care and incorporate relaxation techniques into your routine. Ensure you're staying hydrated, eating balanced meals, and getting enough sleep.

## *Be Careful*

- **Overindulgence:** Avoid excessive spending or partying during celebratory moments.

- **Impulsiveness:** Think carefully before making significant financial or career decisions.
- **Neglecting Details:** As Virgo season begins, pay attention to the finer points in work and personal matters to avoid misunderstandings.

## *Advice*

1. **Celebrate Yourself:** Use the vibrant energy of Leo season to embrace your strengths and take bold steps toward your goals.
2. **Focus on Planning:** As the Virgo season begins, shift your attention to organizing your plans and refining your strategies.
3. **Nurture Relationships:** Invest time in meaningful connections and express gratitude for your loved ones.

## *Additional Tips*

- **Lucky Days:** August 8, 18, and 28 – Perfect for decision-making, creative pursuits, or deepening relationships.
- **Lucky Color:** Sunflower Yellow – This color symbolizes positivity, joy, and self-confidence.
- **Affirmation for August:** *"I shine brightly and align my actions with my purpose, creating joy and success in my life."*

August 2025 is a month of celebration, progress, and grounding for Leo. By balancing bold action with thoughtful planning, you'll navigate this empowering period with confidence and set the stage for long-term success.

# September

September 2025 is a month of grounding, organization, and introspection for Leo. With the Sun in Virgo for most of the month, your focus shifts toward refining your goals, paying attention to details, and strengthening your foundations. As the Sun transitions into Libra later in the month, the energy becomes more balanced and social, encouraging meaningful connections and collaborative efforts. This is an excellent time to find harmony between personal ambitions and relationships.

## *Work*

September offers opportunities for Leos to focus on productivity and long-term planning.

- **Opportunities:** The Virgo energy supports organizing projects, fine-tuning strategies, and addressing overlooked details. Networking during the Libra season later in the month may lead to new opportunities or partnerships.
- **Challenges:** You may feel overwhelmed by the need for perfection or by juggling multiple tasks. Avoid overanalyzing or micromanaging.

**Advice:** Use the Virgo energy to prioritize your tasks and set realistic goals. As Libra season begins, embrace teamwork and collaborative projects to ease the workload and expand your reach.

## *Finance*

Your financial outlook in September emphasizes disciplined spending and cautious planning.

- **Opportunities:** This is a great time to focus on budgeting, saving, and evaluating long-term investments. Financial rewards may come from past efforts or well-thought-out strategies.
- **Challenges:** Avoid impulsive spending, especially on items that aren't aligned with your priorities.

**Advice:** Stick to your budget and reassess your financial goals. Use this month to create a stronger foundation for future growth.

## *Love*

September brings a mix of introspection and harmony to your love life.

- **For Singles:** You may meet someone through work, networking, or mutual connections. However, take your time to build trust and compatibility before diving in.
- **For Those in Relationships:** Focus on deepening emotional intimacy and addressing any lingering

concerns. Open communication and shared activities will strengthen your bond.

**Advice:** Be patient and thoughtful in your interactions. Use the Libra energy later in the month to bring balance and harmony to your relationships.

## *Health*

Health-wise, September encourages Leo to prioritize balance and consistency in wellness routines.

- **Strengths:** The Virgo energy supports creating or refining healthy habits. Activities like meal planning, yoga, or walking will help maintain physical and mental well-being.
- **Challenges:** Stress from work or personal responsibilities may affect your energy levels if not managed effectively.

**Advice:** Incorporate mindfulness practices into your routine to reduce stress. Ensure you're staying hydrated, eating nutritious meals, and getting adequate rest.

## *Be Careful*

- **Overthinking:** Avoid getting bogged down in unnecessary details or perfectionism. Focus on progress over perfection.

- **Neglecting Relationships:** While focusing on work and self-improvement, don't overlook the importance of nurturing your connections.
- **Burnout:** Balance productivity with relaxation to maintain energy and motivation.

## *Advice*

1. **Refine Your Goals:** Use Virgo energy to fine-tune your plans and build a solid foundation for success.
2. **Strengthen Connections:** As Libra season begins, focus on building trust and harmony in personal and professional relationships.
3. **Prioritize Self-Care:** Maintain balance by incorporating relaxation and mindfulness practices into your daily life.

## *Additional Tips*

- **Lucky Days:** September 7, 14, and 23 – Ideal for decision-making, creative projects, or fostering relationships.
- **Lucky Color:** Forest Green – This color enhances growth, balance, and stability.
- **Affirmation for September:** *"I embrace balance and growth, creating harmony and success in all areas of my life."*

September 2025 is a month of grounding and harmony for Leo. By focusing on self-improvement, meaningful relationships, and thoughtful planning, you'll navigate this productive period with confidence and clarity.

# October

October 2025 is a month of balance, collaboration, and introspection for Leo. With the Sun in Libra for most of the month, the focus is on relationships, harmony, and finding equilibrium in your personal and professional life. As the Sun transitions into Scorpio later in the month, the energy deepens, encouraging introspection, emotional growth, and transformation. This is a time to balance your natural boldness with sensitivity, ensuring your actions align with your deeper values.

## *Work*

October highlights teamwork, networking, and strategic planning in Leo's professional life.

- **Opportunities:** Libra Energy supports collaboration and building stronger professional relationships. Mid-month is ideal for resolving conflicts, proposing ideas, or seeking partnerships. The Scorpio influence later in the month helps you focus on complex tasks and long-term goals.
- **Challenges:** You may feel torn between focusing on collaboration and pursuing individual goals. Avoid letting ego or impatience disrupt group dynamics.

**Advice:** Use Libra's harmonious energy to foster teamwork and Scorpio's depth to dive into projects that require focus and strategy. Maintain a diplomatic approach to ensure success.

## *Finance*

Your financial situation in October emphasizes mindful spending and reevaluating financial strategies.

- **Opportunities:** Joint ventures or investments may show positive results. This is also a good time to revisit budgets and refine savings goals.
- **Challenges:** Avoid impulsive spending on luxury items or social events that don't align with your priorities.

**Advice:** Focus on long-term financial security. Use the introspective Scorpio energy to assess your financial habits and make necessary adjustments.

## *Love*

October brings warmth and depth to your love life, with Venus fostering harmony and Scorpio energy enhancing emotional intimacy.

- **For Singles:** Social gatherings, creative activities, or mutual friends may lead to meaningful romantic encounters. Look for connections that resonate on a deeper emotional level.

- **For Those in Relationships:** Focus on building trust and emotional closeness with your partner. Honest communication and shared experiences will strengthen your bond.

**Advice:** Be open about your feelings and attentive to your partner's needs. Use the transformative energy of late October to resolve any lingering issues and deepen your connection.

## *Health*

Health-wise, October encourages Leo to focus on balance and mindfulness.

- **Strengths:** The Libra energy supports maintaining wellness routines, such as balanced nutrition, regular exercise, and relaxation techniques.
- **Challenges:** Stress from work or personal responsibilities may impact your overall energy if not managed carefully.

**Advice:** Incorporate activities that nurture both your body and mind, such as yoga, meditation, or nature walks. Prioritize rest and avoid overexertion to maintain your well-being.

<u>*Be Careful*</u>

- **Overextending:** Don't overcommit to social or professional obligations, as this could lead to stress or burnout.
- **Emotional Reactivity:** Stay calm and grounded during conflicts or emotionally charged situations.
- **Neglecting Self-Care:** Balance your focus on others with attention to your own needs.

<u>*Advice*</u>

1. **Focus on Harmony:** Use Libra energy to foster balance and collaboration in your relationships and professional life.
2. **Embrace Transformation:** As Scorpio season begins, focus on introspection and resolving deeper emotional matters.
3. **Maintain Balance:** Avoid overcommitting by setting boundaries and prioritizing self-care.

<u>*Additional Tips*</u>

- **Lucky Days:** October 10, 18, and 27 – Perfect for creative pursuits, decision-making, or strengthening relationships.
- **Lucky Color:** Burgundy – This color symbolizes passion, depth, and emotional strength.

- **Affirmation for October:** *"I balance action with introspection, creating harmony and meaningful growth in my life."*

October 2025 is a month of balance and transformation for Leo. By focusing on meaningful connections, thoughtful planning, and self-reflection, you'll navigate this dynamic period with confidence and clarity.

# November

November 2025 is a month of introspection, transformation, and emotional depth for Leo. With the Sun in Scorpio during the first part of the month, your focus will be on personal growth, resolving lingering issues, and aligning with your deeper desires. As the Sun transitions into Sagittarius later in the month, the energy lightens, encouraging optimism, exploration, and forward momentum. This is a time to balance inner work with outward action, creating harmony between your ambitions and personal growth.

## *Work*

November presents opportunities for Leos to focus on strategy and take decisive action in their professional life.

- **Opportunities:** The Scorpio energy supports diving into complex tasks, research, or problem-solving. Mid-month is ideal for proposing new ideas, refining long-term goals, or pursuing leadership opportunities.
- **Challenges:** Emotional intensity or unresolved workplace dynamics may create temporary obstacles. Maintain professionalism and diplomacy.

**Advice:** Use the introspective energy of early November to reassess your career objectives. The Sagittarius influence later in the month will help you step forward with renewed confidence and optimism.

## *Finance*

Your financial outlook in November encourages careful planning and thoughtful decision-making.

- **Opportunities:** Investments made earlier may start showing positive results. This is also a good time to plan for year-end financial responsibilities or future savings goals.
- **Challenges:** Avoid impulsive financial decisions or spending excessively on luxury items or social events.

**Advice:** Focus on financial security by prioritizing budgeting and long-term planning. Seek advice if considering significant investments or changes.

## *Love*

November brings emotional depth and growth to your love life.

- **For Singles:** This is a powerful time for meaningful connections. You may meet someone who

resonates with your values and emotional depth through shared activities or social circles.
- **For Those in Relationships:** Focus on nurturing emotional intimacy and resolving past misunderstandings with your partner. The Sagittarius energy later in the month encourages playful and adventurous bonding.

**Advice:** Be open and honest about your feelings. Use the transformative energy of Scorpio season to strengthen trust and the lighthearted energy of Sagittarius to add excitement.

## *Health*

Health-wise, November encourages Leo to focus on emotional and physical balance.

- **Strengths:** The Scorpio energy inspires you to engage in activities that nurture both your mind and body, such as yoga, meditation, or journaling.
- **Challenges:** Stress from emotional or professional matters may lead to fatigue if not managed effectively.

**Advice:** Prioritize self-care by incorporating relaxation techniques and maintaining consistent wellness routines. Ensure you're staying hydrated and getting enough rest to recharge.

<u>*Be Careful*</u>

- **Overanalyzing:** Avoid dwelling on past mistakes or letting unresolved issues cloud your focus.
- **Impulsiveness:** Think carefully before making major decisions, particularly in financial or personal matters.
- **Neglecting Balance:** Balance introspection with social engagement to avoid feeling isolated.

<u>*Advice*</u>

1. **Focus on Transformation:** Use Scorpio energy to resolve deeper issues and realign with your long-term goals.
2. **Embrace Optimism:** As Sagittarius season begins, focus on exploring new opportunities and maintaining a positive outlook.
3. **Maintain Balance:** Balance emotional depth with moments of lightness and joy to create harmony in your life.

<u>*Additional Tips*</u>

- **Lucky Days:** November 8, 16, and 28 – Ideal for introspection, decision-making, or creative pursuits.
- **Lucky Color:** Deep Purple – This color symbolizes transformation, intuition, and strength.

- **Affirmation for November:** *"I embrace growth and balance, creating harmony and success in all areas of my life."*

November 2025 is a month of transformation and exploration for Leo. By focusing on self-improvement, meaningful connections, and thoughtful planning, you'll navigate this powerful period with confidence and clarity.

# December

December 2025 is a month of reflection, celebration, and preparation for Leo. With the Sun in Sagittarius during the first part of the month, you'll feel inspired to connect with others, explore new opportunities, and embrace your adventurous spirit. As the Sun transitions into Capricorn later in December, the focus shifts to grounding, organization, and setting the stage for a successful 2026. This month offers the perfect balance between enjoying the festive season and planning for the future.

## *Work*

December brings opportunities for Leos to reflect on achievements and set new goals for the coming year.

- **Opportunities:** The Sagittarius energy supports networking, brainstorming, and exploring new career paths. Mid-month is ideal for wrapping up ongoing projects and evaluating your progress. The Capricorn energy later in the month encourages disciplined planning for long-term success.
- **Challenges:** Balancing work responsibilities with personal commitments during the holiday season may feel overwhelming.

**Advice:** Use the dynamic Sagittarius energy to think big and the grounded Capricorn influence to refine your strategies. Stay organized to manage your workload effectively.

### *Finance*

Your financial situation in December emphasizes mindful spending and year-end planning.

- **Opportunities:** Bonuses, rewards, or financial gains from past efforts may provide a boost. This is a good time to reassess your budget and plan for future expenses or investments.
- **Challenges:** Holiday spending on gifts, travel, or social activities could strain your finances if not managed carefully.

**Advice:** Stick to a budget and prioritize long-term financial stability over short-term indulgences. Consider delaying major purchases until you've reviewed your financial goals.

### *Love*

December is a warm and affectionate month for Leo's love life, with Venus enhancing connection and emotional depth.

- **For Singles:** Social events, festive gatherings, or travel opportunities may lead to new romantic connections. Be open to meeting people who share your adventurous spirit and optimism.
- **For Those in Relationships:** Focus on quality time with your partner, reflecting on your journey together, and planning for the future. Shared celebrations will bring you closer and deepen your bond.

**Advice:** Use Sagittarius energy to add excitement and spontaneity to your love life. As Capricorn season begins, focus on building stability and mutual understanding.

## *Health*

Health-wise, December encourages Leo to balance activity and relaxation during the festive season.

- **Strengths:** Your energy levels will remain steady, making it a good time to enjoy social activities, fitness routines, or creative pursuits.
- **Challenges:** Overindulgence in food, drink, or late nights may affect your well-being if not moderated.

**Advice:** Practice moderation and prioritize self-care amidst celebrations. Incorporate light exercise and mindfulness practices to stay grounded and refreshed.

## *Be Careful*

- **Overspending:** Avoid letting the excitement of the holidays lead to unnecessary financial stress.
- **Neglecting Rest:** Ensure you're balancing social commitments with adequate downtime to recharge.
- **Rushed Decisions:** Take your time when planning for the year ahead; avoid making impulsive commitments or resolutions.

## *Advice*

1. **Celebrate Progress:** Reflect on your achievements and express gratitude for the growth you've experienced in 2025.
2. **Plan:** Use the Capricorn energy to set realistic and inspiring goals for 2026.
3. **Nurture Connections:** Strengthen your relationships by spending meaningful time with loved ones and sharing your appreciation for them.

<u>***Additional Tips***</u>

- **Lucky Days:** December 9, 19, and 28 – Perfect for reflecting, planning, or celebrating special moments.
- **Lucky Color:** Ruby Red – This color symbolizes passion, energy, and joy.
- **Affirmation for December:** *"I celebrate my journey and prepare for a future filled with purpose, joy, and success."*

December 2025 is a month of celebration and preparation for Leo. By balancing festivity with reflection and thoughtful planning, you'll end the year on a high note and set the stage for a fulfilling 2026.

# Good Luck For 2025